Chakra Balancing

Davina DeSilver

Copyright © 2013 Davina DeSilver

All rights reserved.

ISBN: 1482599651
ISBN-13: 9781482599657

DEDICATION

To all those who believed in me & showed me love

And to all those that didn't & showed me a better way

To Kirsty & Kim
Love is a light that shines, touching hearts & holding hands with our spirits forever.

CONTENTS

Preface

1	Can You Talk the Language of Energy?	1
2	It's Not Just About Balance	7
3	The Root Chakra	12
4	The Sacral Chakra	23
5	Can You Trust Your Gut?	31
6	Closed or Open to Love?	39
7	What's Your Throat Really Saying?	47
8	The Third Eye. Psychic, Crazy or Wise?	53
9	Are You Suffering From a Sense of Disconnection?	61
10	How's Your Aura?	67

PREFACE

This book came about after having been asked over the years to put down in writing what I see, feel and interpret with regards to the energy of the body. When I have given talks and presentations, people have been delighted with the way I put the information across. I like to keep it real, practical and down to earth.

Initially I found it tricky to decide where to start. So I have broken it down into specific areas. This particular book is to help those relatively new to the chakras, get a better understanding of them and to give simple ways to start balancing and working with your own amazing energy.

Many books on the subject can get very complicated and far too ethereal. Some people have told me that they find that quite intimidating or just too hard to believe, so they end up dismissing the entire topic.

In this book, I give a brief overview of the chakras and then we dive right in to a chapter devoted to each of the main seven energy centres.

You'll discover the signs of a healthy functioning chakra, as well as signs of imbalance and ways to bring balance back to each chakra. It's perfect for you if you like the straight forward, no nonsense approach. If you are relatively new to the topic, I have tried to keep it easy to follow.

Then we touch on the aura as a whole and in the resource section, you'll find links to further articles and MP3 recordings to start balancing your chakras today. I'll be adding to that resource page over time, so check back regularly.

I'm really excited to be working on my next book which will share with people how I read auras, so you can learn to start doing the same thing for yourself and your friends, maybe even adding it as a service you offer to clients.

Working with the energy of the body is a great way of improving and harnessing your own psychic ability and your spiritual awareness.

About the Author

Davina DeSilver is a Reiki Master and hypnotherapist, she specialised in past life regression therapy.

She has worked with some of the latest aura technology and has spent a lot of time working with the human spirit. She has facilitated development groups with other psychics and mediums too.

"I find the whole area of auras and chakras a hugely fascinating subject and never fail to be amazed at what can be seen and revealed there. Basically everything links to and *is* energy, the names we end up giving things is just language!"

1 CAN YOU TALK THE LANGUAGE OF ENERGY?

An Introduction to the Chakras:

Chakra is an ancient Sanskrit term, it's translated meaning is 'spinning disc' or 'wheel'. More often than not, when we are talking about the chakras of the human body, we tend to be referring to the main seven chakras of the human energy system. (There are more, but for simplicity we will focus on the main seven here).

Despite the ancient unveiling and naming of the chakras, it has been a relatively recent discovery that each of the major chakras resides very close to an important nerve plexus or centre, within the body.

It's important to keep in mind that the chakras are not things you can see or touch, they are not part of your physical body but they *are* part of your energetic body. To me, they are doorways, connecting your conscious and subconscious minds, as well as connecting your energetic and physical body.

The healers and seers of ancient times perceived that these seven major energy hubs or centres, were positioned along the human spine, from the very bottom vertebra, right to the topmost point of the head. They described the energy at these points as spinning. Similar to the motion you see where two volumes of water converge and a whirlpool is created.

The locations of the seven main Chakras are:

- The Base or Root Chakra - The base of the spine
- The Sacral or Second Chakra - The lower abdomen, about a hand width from your navel
- The Third Chakra or Solar Plexus - Resides around the navel and slightly above it
- The Fourth or Heart Chakra - Obviously this is located in the chest area
- The Fifth or Throat Chakra - This energy centre is situated at the throat, and affects the neck region as a whole
- The Sixth Chakra or Third Eye -Located between and slightly above the eyebrows
- The Seventh or Crown Chakra - This uppermost Chakra is positioned at the top of the head

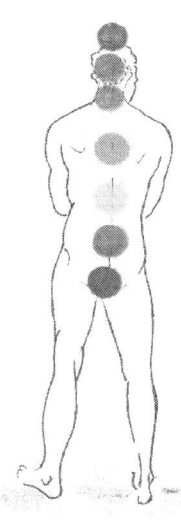

They may not be tangible nor something you have spent a lot of time thinking about but you can certainly become more aware of the existence of the chakra energies. You can become more sensitive to how they feel and then go on to interpret the energetic signals they are constantly giving out.

Every one of the seven chakras vibrates at a unique frequency; its own particular resonance. One of the ways we distinguish them most easily is by colour.

- Red is the colour of the Root Chakra
- Orange for the Sacral Chakra
- Yellow for the Third Chakra/Solar Plexus
- Green for the Heart Chakra
- Blue for the Throat Chakra
- Indigo for the Sixth Chakra/Third Eye
- Violet for the Seventh/Crown Chakra

The energy of the human body is constantly communicating and therefore has a language. It is a language we can all converse in subconsciously. When you can *consciously* understand and communicate with it, then you are in a position to know yourself at a much deeper level, using and directing energy to sustain and improve your general health and wellbeing.

The energy flows from the main centres along minuscule channels, each nourishing and feeding particular areas of the body. Each centre is also associated with the endocrine glands, these regulate many of the main functioning systems of your body, working directly with the hormones. The types of functions affected are: your general energy levels, respiration, reproduction, overall growth and development.

You may have heard about the chakras being out of alignment or balance, maybe even closed. They are constantly regulating your energy, attempting a state of homeostasis, just as the physical body does. Your energetic 'body' is doing the same, it wants a balanced and stable sense of equilibrium. It will strive to maintain a sense of balance as best it can. Being in balance is the optimum healthy state.

The chakras can reveal themselves as being out of balance in a variety of ways. They may spin very slowly, almost unevenly, they may run very fast. The energy can feel weak or may be backing up, coming to a head. A bit like most things in life, we can get away with it for a while. Having an out of balance chakra may not appear to be too significant or important. But as in life, everything does have an effect and compensations will be made, energy may be taken from other sources, and other areas may start to be affected.

Our energy system is similar to our immune system, it can be strong or weak, and any point in between! It is constantly working for our optimum performance and protection. It is possible and in my opinion, more than likely, that a weaker chakra centre is where a physical symptom or problem is going to find it easiest to take hold. It may be in the form of an illness or disease or stress and tension or even an accident and injury.

Metaphysically speaking, areas of the body reveal psychosomatic symptoms and triggers, which can reveal the underlying implications of what is really going on. This is intricately connected with your subconscious thoughts, what your subconscious <u>believes</u> to be true and the subsequent messages it is giving your body. When our minds take hold of something as true, regardless of whether it actually **is** a truth or not, it sets a chain of actions in motion, to reinforce that thought and make it a concrete reality.

It's not just your mind that the chakras connect to. They are also in constant communication with your mental health and emotional wellbeing, not to mention the spiritual aspect of your being. They can reveal so much about us, on so many levels. Regular attention to the chakras and your energy system as a whole can help you achieve a much better level of overall health and a sense of holistic wellbeing.

One thing is a given. Your energy speaks the truth - it doesn't lie. It doesn't smooth over the cracks or say what it thinks you might want to hear - it is quietly broadcasting 24 hours a day in subtle ways - and what it communicates is always the truth.

This is one of the reasons I love energy work so much - it's a bit like working with animals, it is what it is and it does what it does. It is very pure and simple, if there is an imbalance or weakness, it will show it. The magic is in deciphering what it is revealing and that requires an honest and open mind.

In this book, we cover a general, broad overview of the main energy centres and indicators of what it would feel like to be in balance for each chakra. We also highlight some of the most common signs and symptoms of imbalance. Then you'll find there are a few suggestions of simple and practical ways to bring balance back to each one of your chakras.

By the time you've finished, you will be well on your way to learning to speak the language of energy. I've deliberately kept it short, to the point and easy to read, so you can get started right away.

2 IT'S NOT JUST ABOUT BALANCE

Tip the Energy Scales in Your Favour

Don't waste your time on a one - off balance. It's simply not enough.

Lots of people think they are helping themselves by getting into the chakras and think that the odd chakra balance or energy treatment is going to do the job. Just as one trip to the hairdresser won't keep your style looking good for long, neither will the odd half-hearted energy balance. But don't be put off either. There are a great many simple yet effective things you can do and probably to a degree already are doing that can really help your energy system.

The more you make things simple and easy, the more likely you are at being able to sustain it and reap the long term benefits. If you can also make your energy work enjoyable, then the more likely it is you'll find time to fit it into your busy schedule. So then it becomes a part of your regular routine.

The chakras are an integral part of your health. To remain physically healthy you need to eat and act healthily - it is exactly the same with your energetic health. For optimum effect incorporate chakra balancing, breath work or meditating as a part of your regular daily or weekly routine. It shouldn't be a chore as it can be an extremely enjoyable and relaxing, totally therapeutic process! You certainly don't want to be too compulsive or regimental about it either, energy work needs to flow and be fluid. It should be a natural and enjoyable part of your week, that's why I like to include practical and simple methods as they are far more likely to get done.

Not many of us live our lives in balance all the time, floating on a lovely fluffy cloud just above 'real world land'. No, we live in the modern world, with all the wonderful things it brings as well as all the not so wonderful. We have demands on our time, our energy, our pockets and our patience. Keep things as real and practical and as easy to do as you can. To start with, try swapping 30 minutes of TV time for a meditation or relaxation class. The benefits to your body can be immediate.

In a deep state of relaxation, the mind can be so receptive and immensely powerful. It is a direct route to tap into our amazing potential of healing and creativity. Successful business people, sports men and women the world over, use the power of their mind to achieve all sorts of amazing things in their lives. A great many people have healed themselves of all manner of different illnesses and diseases. You don't need to wait until you're unwell to harness this power.

We all have the ability and the potential. For many of us though, it can seem counter intuitive to take time out from our busy lives and if we don't see an immediate effect we decide it's not working and go back to old habits and routines. We get comfortable in our discomfort. It doesn't have to be that way.

Harness the power of your core, your inner self and your chakra energy to find the clarity of thought, the peace of mind and the wisdom to live your life more fulfilled, happy and at ease than you ever imagined was possible. Just make it more likely to happen by establishing new, fun habits that feed and nourish you. Things that balance your energy and positively feed it, without you having to think too much about it.

Learn to speak the language of energy and understand what it is trying to tell you.

Chakra Energy - Where Does it Come From?

There is energy all around us, in everything we can see and in everything we can't. There's energy in the trees, in plants, in our lights and buildings. There's energy in nature herself, trees have a different energy to mountains, the sea has a different energy to earth. Many people are familiar with crystals and can appreciate that they each have their own unique energy too. Everything has its own special frequency, even every individual plant and flower. It is this energy that makes homeopathy and aromatherapy so successful. So already you can see we are swimming in a universal soup of energy, we can't not be affected by it. This is how we are all connected. Not joined at the hip but swimming in the same big pond.

It doesn't stop there; each and every organ in the body and every illness have a different energy too. It's not just your physical movements and actions that have a frequency and an energetic effect, your words and thoughts do too.

Everything has its own unique frequency and energy vibration

This might seem a little hard to take but consider how you feel when you hear a beautiful hymn or a Christmas carol being sung. It lifts your spirit and makes you feel good inside. Now how does it feel when you hear harsh words, it usually sparks a completely different reaction inside. It doesn't feel good at all and it might even spark a fearful reaction in you. There is energy in those words, in their feeling and emotion. Emotions are our most powerful energy transmitters. We are reacting on an energetic level all the time. The chakras are our energy hubs; they constantly take in this energy and release it out.

As you might expect, some things are good for your energy and some things are not so great. Some things feed you and some detract from you. You will already have a pretty good idea of what does and doesn't work for you, even if you haven't outwardly acknowledged it before. You may even have noticed that some places feel comfortable and ok with you and some seem to make you feel on edge or your skin crawl. What is attractive and appealing to one, will not necessarily be the same for the next person. It is precisely because the energies are continually fluctuating, in and out that we need to understand them better. If we can work in harmony for more of the time and less against the flow, the better off we all will be.

If you can imagine the exchange of energy is as vital and as integral as breathing - in and out, in and out, 24- 7,then you can appreciate that a one - off energy balance won't do much good. Find ways that you know work for you, try some of the things I mention in this book, some you'll like and be drawn to and some you won't. What matters is, you find what works for you, and the things you know feed your energy, without having to drastically alter your life or abstain from the modern world and all the wonders it has to offer.

3 THE ROOT CHAKRA

Sex, Money & Fear

The Root Chakra, also known as the First or Base Chakra is fundamental to your presence here on earth. It is intrinsically linked to your core physical health and your energy levels as a whole. Many people overlook this chakra, particularly those that have a spiritual bias around the topic of energy. Often they will push aside the lower chakras in the vain hope that connecting more with the upper chakras will make them more enlightened.

However it is precisely these lower energy centres that enable you to function, to live life, to stand upright and to fully inhabit your physical body. Without these you may just as well be a ghost. To me spirituality is not about dissociating from life, it's about embracing it. Dancing in the knowledge that my spirit is alive and having the conscious awareness that what I am living, I am creating. You need a certain degree of stamina and backbone to dance that dance - welcome to the domain of the Base Chakra.

Each of the chakras resonates to a different colour frequency and here at the base, it is red. The colour is used to bring balance and healing. In future books in this series, I cover the meaning of colours more deeply. The relevant colours are often drawn into the chakras to help bring balance and renewed energy, especially in chakra healing. Often a crystal of the same colour might be placed over the centre or visualised and can be very effective.

Each energy centre also connects with the area of the body they are located in, so here we are talking about the lowermost point of the spine, the perineum, in fact the entire spine and skeletal system, right down to your feet. This is all about your core fundamentals, needed to survive. So it includes, your blood, your bones and your internal sex organs.

Apart from the physical attributes it is also linked to your sense of **survival and security** and your **fight or flight** responses. It's about how you stand up for yourself, your backbone, your ability to 'stand on your own two feet'. It encompasses your mental and emotional attitude in these areas too. Although we are all connected, this is about you, your energy, your unique expression of consciousness.

Relating this to modern life, take some time to ask yourself some questions "What makes me feel safe?" It is no doubt in some way connected to home, family, core relationships and stability, which today probably includes your financial security. Money, or the lack of it can be a major concern. If you can't pay your bills and are always struggling to make ends meet that tension and anxiety will show in the Root Chakra energy. Any threat to your home - your 'base' will show up, it's not just money but if the atmosphere at home is tense, if there are arguments and rifts in the family or at work, they will all be reflected here.

You may notice physical symptoms, equally you may recognise some of the more mental or emotional aspects of stress and tension. The energetic imbalance will reveal itself in one way or another. The way you think about money and your attitude to risk in general will show up in the Root Chakra to some degree - as to whether or not you are consciously aware of it, is another thing entirely!

Your Sexual Centre

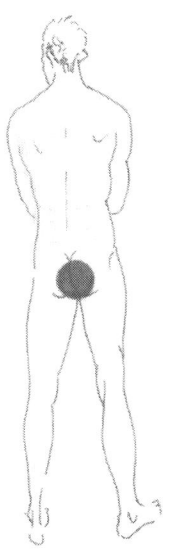

The Root or 1st Chakra opens out and downwards from the top of the legs down to the earth, in a spiralling motion. It sits right at your sexual centre and is associated not just with the physical organs themselves but with your feelings around your sexuality. How comfortable you are with it, your sexual health in general as much as your feelings about pleasure and performance.

For example, impotence can be attributed as being a sign of imbalance in the Root Chakra. It is suggested impotence not only has the more obvious symptoms but can be psychological and have deep roots in the individual's sense of self worth and security. Pile on top of this the pressure of 'performance', then it is easy to understand how this could easily become an ever increasing spiral of let down and self recrimination.

The same can be said with regards to any problems directly associated to your most private organs and intimate functions. It is absolutely these that the Base Chakra and its' energy incorporate.

That does not mean to say that by bringing the chakra to balance once or twice you'll solve any deeper problems. If things have a psychological root, they require honesty and time for reflection and integration; they do not tend to respond to quick fixes. An attitude to improving the balance of the energy here at the base, as well as honestly dealing with any associated psychological issues will bring about much improvement though.

The chakras indicate our deep inner feelings, our insecurities or fears. When we are ready, we can deal with them effectively. This doesn't mean just using energy work and visualisation - it's not an either - or situation. We can use energy alongside conventional health and healing, incorporating the best of both, having a holistic and balanced approach to life in general.   The chakra energy can be a very reliable way of unlocking some of the secrets your subconscious has been tightly holding on to - they most definitely hold the key to better understanding.

The Base Chakra is the first place to start with **any** physical body issues or concerns you might have.

Balance at the Base Chakra

This chakra is not just about your core needs, your overall health and vitality; it's also about your ability to manifest. It deals with the power you have to make things happen, your drive to succeed and to live a life you enjoy. In harmony with this energy centre you enjoy a sense of being the creator of your world, an active, vibrant being, living life in flow, dealing with challenges and creating new experiences.

In balance with the Base Chakra you'll recognise:

- Feeling 'good in your skin', happy with who you are
- Feeling 'present' and grounded
- Feeling content with life in general, particularly with regards to home, finance, family and your close relationships
- Good physical health and a sense of awareness about life
- A quiet confidence in your ability to make things happen and to enjoy carving out the life you want
- A good work/life balance

Indicators of Imbalance:

As this energy centre is so integral to your physical body, *any* illness can bring about an imbalance. However, there are certain regions that this chakra particularly governs;

- Any bone disorders or general problems with the spine and skeletal system
- Foot and leg problems
- Sexual issues, physical, mental and emotional
- Blood irregularities or disorders of any kind
- Anxiety, panic attacks
- Any anger or aggression problems, from showing bouts of uncontrollable anger, right down to being too passive, possibly finding yourself the victim on a regular basis
- A feeling that whatever you touch seems to go wrong and things just never seem to work out for you.

The chakra energy can be expressed and felt in many ways. Imbalance is the term we use to indicate a lack of harmony and generally there tends to be two broad variations; overactive or underactive.

Underactive Base Chakra Energy:

Typically you might notice:

- A general lethargy about life
- Having no energy, no zest, you may even say "my get up and go has got up and gone"
- People tend to boss you about, even to the point of abuse and bullying
- Feeling anxious, more so than normal, or about things that didn't used to bother you that much
- You may have some eating habits that are not healthy, with a tendency to be underweight
- Feeling a bit of a loner, not part of many groups, a feeling you don't fit in with other people much
- Impotence or weak and irregular periods

Overactive Base Chakra Energy:

- A tendency to easily put on weight
- Feeling sluggish, heavier as if you're generally slowing down
- Hoarding - holding on to things, sometimes there's a sense of greediness
- Overspending or working long hours, becoming very materialistic
- Angry outbursts, things seem to come to a pretty explosive head at times

Naturally, this list is by no means exclusive but it does provide a starting point to give you a flavour of the nature of the Base Chakra energy.

Practical Ways to Balance the Base Chakra

This chakra is aligned with the element of earth. So to bring balance it is helpful to keep that in mind. You want activities that connect with that element in some way. A good place to start is the food you eat. You don't have to diet or bring in any tough regime but pay a little more attention to the foods you eat and where you get them from. So much of what is good for us, can seem a little too simple, so we don't tend to do them.

Can you incorporate a few more vegetables into your weekly menus, more organic produce, more raw foods? Juicing is a brilliant way to get more of the good stuff in a tasty way. Especially the veggies you normally avoid, when they're all juiced up, they taste great! Widen the scope of the vegetables and grains you buy. Not only will be you be helping yourself but if you're cooking for the family, you will be helping them too.

How about exercise, are you getting enough? Have you settled into routines? Is there a specific set of muscles that you need or want to work on? Exercise doesn't have to be a chore, find ways to make it fun. Join groups, try something new. There's no need to sign up for a marathon, a daily walk around the block, when you know it's feeding your energy can make all the difference.

Being outside is especially good for this chakra, particularly if it involves touching the ground in some way. It doesn't matter if it's running, cycling, walking, gardening or rock climbing. Yoga of course, is great for all of the chakras and there are specific poses to stimulate each energy centre.

Try getting your hands dirty, get creative. Gardening is great, so is pottery or woodwork, anything using your hands to shape and mould things. This works with your energy to manifest and make things happen. It is a physical and tangible way of connecting you to the energy of creating and connection.

Everything we do on a physical level has an impact on other levels too, mentally, emotionally *and* spiritually. The physical activity itself may seem trivial, but with awareness you can rest in the knowledge that it is having a much deeper impact. As you embrace such activities and techniques, you become more mindful to everything you do and slowly you notice some very positive changes.

If you like the odd treatment, try reflexology. It's a great general therapy and it is particularly good for the base chakra as it is time spent specifically focused on the feet. It is so easy for us to ignore and forget just how hard our feet work, so a little bit of TLC can work wonders. Also the reflexologist will be working on other areas of the body and imbalances that make themselves known, as the feet are like mini maps of the entire body.

Where possible, when you are outside, go barefoot for a while and really absorb in the energy from the ground beneath you. This works really well once you've listened to a few visualisations and can work with the imagery in your mind.

As with all the energy centres, to bring a sense of calm you need to relax, not the in front of the TV kind of relax, but a deep relaxation that allows your mind, muscles and fibres to feel heavenly. If meditation is not for you or too much to start with, try a short guided visualisation. The words will keep your mind busy and some will even talk you through simple processes of muscle relaxation. If you check out the resource page, there's a link to some I've recorded you can easily download. If you do nothing else, try and make relaxation a habit as it has so many health benefits, but again we tend to struggle with the idea of doing less to achieve more.

It's easy to get overwhelmed, just try one or two things and cultivate them as new habits, then introduce more. Also try to be less of a multi-tasker, personally I have found this really difficult. We hear so much about how good it is to multitask but often it would produce better results if we tried to do less and concentrated more. It's so easy for our focus to get pulled away and it's that power of focus that also helps us to manifest, create things and get them done.

Give up the need to be perfect. Lighten up on how you treat and talk to yourself. The Root Chakra relates to our early, formative years and on a psychological level this can be when we take on a lot of beliefs and behaviours. (Which when you question them as an adult no longer fit).

What you may find is that you can be quite hard on yourself, especially with regards to how you talk to yourself - I often liken it to talking to your best friend or your own children - if you're not talking to yourself in the same way you would talk to them, then maybe there is room for improvement. This all connects to your self awareness and self esteem. Even if you aren't saying such things out loud: "you fool", "how stupid", "you never get it right", "you always say the wrong thing" - they could be forming a consistent part of your *internal* conversations and are often much more insidious and damaging than you might first imagine.

The important thing to remember is that your energy is all about **you** . How you find balance may not be how the next person finds balance, even if they are working on the same chakra. We are all similar yet our bodies and our energy are very, very unique and specific to each individual. I can only give you areas to consider here, so if one thing doesn't fit with you, then try something else on the list - as we each find our own way.

This is not about pleasing anyone else nor the right or wrong way to do things - there is no right or wrong - only what works for you.

4 THE SACRAL CHAKRA

Are Your Passions & Desires in Balance?

The next chakra we meet up from the bottom of the spine is the Sacral Chakra. This energy centre is connected to your emotions and your creativity in general. It encompasses your relationships, your sensuality and even your appetite. It's all about the things that repel you and attract you, basically your likes, dislikes, your passions and desires.

This is the emotional centre and as emotions are very powerful things, this is quite a powerhouse and is an energy centre that can easily be pulled out of balance. As they run so deeply and powerfully, emotions can be hard for us to acknowledge, let alone effectively express and release them.

They may not make much sense at times, but our feelings do need to be aired. It has been said that unexpressed emotions can often be the trigger underlying many illnesses and diseases. This is the base behind psychosomatic illness and metaphysical literature in general aligns with this theory too. Every illness has a story to tell.

In Balance with the Sacral Chakra:

This is about the people and things you love, the things you draw closer to you and the things you push away. This is your pleasure centre. The Second Chakra resonates with the colour orange and the overriding essence of the energy here has a much more fluid and sensual feel than the base. Although both chakras relate to sex, the first energy centre was more about the physical act and instinctive drive. The Sacral Chakra is much more about sensuality, your feelings, your senses and desires, all the intangible aspects of sexuality and the emotive power behind our ability to create.

In harmony with the Sacral Chakra you'll enjoy:

- An ability to flow with life, to accept change without the need for extremes
- A feeling of emotional stability and intelligence, for yourself and others
- Recognising your own healthy boundaries
- Satisfying your own needs and wants, sharing with others whilst acknowledging your own values
- A sense of enjoying what you do, whether that is at work or home

Signs of Imbalance:

It is relatively easy for this chakra to be out of balance and you may discover that you tend to overindulge in the things that seem to bring you pleasure and all the while you still feel hollow on the inside. It doesn't matter what form the indulgence takes; from food to sex, to alcohol and drugs. It might even be a need for thrill seeking or extreme sports and pursuits.

It's like the adrenaline rush takes over and you can almost be beside yourself. This centre is also one that can seem to stagnate, especially when we talk of creativity, whether that be writers block or the ability to conceive.

Underactive Sacral Chakra Energy:

- You might suffer from soreness or stiffness in the lower back and hips
- You might be so resistant to change that you have quite fixed rituals and habits
- You may avoid social activity and withdraw from relationships
- You might feel like you don't have any particular wants and passion is not a word that you would use about yourself
- Infertility problems, IBS, weak menstrual cycle, issues with the reproductive organs/system
- You might have a gnawing sense of dissatisfaction about life in general, without being able to put your finger on anything specific

Overactive Sacral Chakra Energy - You'll Recognise

- An addictive tendency to one or more; smoking, food, drink, drugs, sex, unhealthy relationships
- A tendency to put on weight around the mid section and hips, overweight in general
- Maintaining healthy boundaries can be a challenge
- Mood swings may be common, you may be up one minute and down the next
- Unhealthy co - dependent relationships

Practical Ways to Balance the Sacral Chakra:

This chakra is associated with the element of water and this is all about flow. To be in harmony with this energy centre you want to be able to flow with life, changing course when needed but able to steer that course. This is not about getting washed away in everybody else's flow. It's about being in touch with you - knowing what you do and don't like, knowing what and who is and isn't good for you. It's about knowing what you want to achieve and aim for.

It's about healthy boundaries, knowing limits and realistic expectations. It's a beautiful balance; pleasing yourself, without dominating or being selfish towards others. It comes down to that well known sentiment that in order to love someone else, you need to love yourself first.

There's an awareness here about the natural cycles of life, when to nurture, when to rest and when to reap the rewards. We can enjoy a better degree of balance in our lives if we can incorporate pleasure in our lives, in as many different areas as we can. If we enjoy our work, our home life and genuinely enjoy being with our friends and acquaintances then life feels good. But so many people find themselves in jobs they hate, in a home that doesn't inspire them and with people that drain their time and energy.

Working with the chakras requires regular reality checks. Do you really like spending time with your current social circle, is there another group of people who might be more like minded? Is there anything you can do to make your home life more relaxing and pleasurable? Are there jobs you've been putting off, that if they just got done, it would make you feel that bit better? Without any pleasure what does life become - what do *we* become?

A great way of working with the Sacral Chakra is to get back in touch with your own body, especially the regions of the body it relates to - the lower abdomen and back. In our working days, many of us don't get to exercise this area very much, as a result we can suffer from reduced movement and poor posture. Include a few simple exercises like hip rotations into your day. One of the most enjoyable things can be dancing, especially belly dancing, in fact that sums up the general feel of this chakra - fluid, sensual movements. It's not just about sex and sensuality but also the fluid motion and mobility of the spine itself. Just as our muscles can become tense and rigid, so it is with the feel of the energy here at times, people can become taut, harsh and almost brittle and this energy centre is always affected by that.

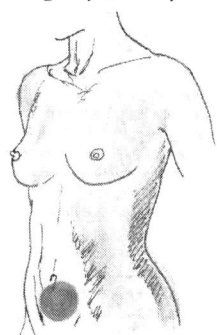

A great deal of yoga poses can be of immense help with this chakra and Pilates concentrates on your core muscles and is very beneficial too. The Bridge pose is a great exercise to increase suppleness. When you give the exercise a go, make sure you engage your brain in the action too as it makes the movements so much more intense and worthwhile. You'll find you can almost stretch further and achieve more if you visualise the muscles moving and gently easing out as you make the tiny movements required to hold the pose.

We are all aware of the need to drink water and it is particularly relevant to this centre. Again, time for a reality check here, how many glasses a day are you managing to drink - just because we know it's a good idea to do something, it doesn't mean to say we're actually managing to do it!

When it comes to your intimate nature and your sexuality you may want to explore your thoughts and feelings. Are there certain concerns you have or niggling worries. Is there something you have been putting off dealing with? If talking to someone about it doesn't appeal, try writing about it. Start a simple journal, for your eyes only. There's a great book by Julia Cameron, The Artist's Way, you'll find links in the resource section, which recommends writing as a way of releasing any blocked creativity, it's not just for artists but for all of us as by the nature of being human, we are all creative.

Are you over-shy or inhibited and does this then have an effect on your self confidence? Sexually confident people do tend to have a certain charisma and aura about them.

You might want to look at your own self respect and how you treat yourself on a daily level. What is your own self talk like? Many people are oblivious to the sorts of words and labels they habitually apply to themselves and they consider that if they are not actually self harming then things can't be too bad. But when they pause to really consider what they are saying to themselves, they realise that it is not conducive to getting the best out of themselves and it's often not supportive or nurturing either.

Take time to recall what your hopes were as a child, what did you dream of doing or becoming? Is there a hobby you could take up now that would at least satisfy a part of that young urge? Again, it can seem like there is no time for such things but if you want to improve the energy here in this chakra, then you need to find the time!

Can you receive gifts and compliments well? Pay more attention to your core relationships at home and at work. Try viewing them as if you were surveying the scene rather than being part of it. This subtle shift can be very enlightening, regarding the part you play in the dramas of your life. Bringing more awareness to our relationships can help uncover if there are any improvements or adjustments that might be made.

The Sacral Chakra is about feeding yourself well - physically speaking and energetically speaking. It's about your appetite for food *and* your appetite for life and finding the balance so you neither starve nor over indulge. This is about enjoying the flow of life, being able to accept changes as you know that just around the corner there'll be something else you'll love and enjoy just as much. How do you know that? Because you know you listen to your own heart, your wants and needs and know that to be able to give of your best you have to be properly nourished and feel alive on every level.

A crystal often used to bring balance to this centre is Citrine, not just because of its similar colour but because of its affinity with the natural flow of emotional energy.

5 CAN YOU TRUST YOUR GUT?

The Solar Plexus

The Third Chakra is your Solar Plexus. This is all about how you regulate your energy, your will power and your focus. It's about your strength, your character, the energy you put into things, it's the motivating chakra of drive and momentum, to bring your ideas and hopes into reality. It's not uncommon to see this chakra out of balance and this can often be seen in people who are domineering and controlling, the converse being your energy is zapped from this centre if you are the one being controlled and dominated.

As we progress through the chakras, you'll see it's a bit like taking a journey; each stop builds on the last. The First Chakra is about your arrival, your immediate and instinctive needs to survive. The Second Chakra introduced your individual wants and needs, your likes and dislikes, here, the Solar Plexus provides the power to make them happen. In future books you'll see that same journey also unfolds on a spiritual level through the chakras, just on a bigger, more expansive scale. But for our purposes here, I'll try and keep focused on the practical more immediate elements and attributes of the physical, mental and emotional levels of your energy system.

Although this is the power centre, it can unfortunately be very easy for us to assign our power to others, sometimes willingly and sometimes inadvertently. The trouble is as you allow others to feed on your reserves of energy, then you can find yourself lacking the drive and impetus to even remember your goals, let alone have the energy to do anything about them. You can then find yourself with an attitude that there's little you can do to make things better, believing goals and dreams are for other people. You can become cynical and resign yourself to that's just the way the world is and settle to just accept the cards that have been dealt to you. To me it's like losing a bit of your spirit.

The Solar Plexus is associated with the colour yellow and the element it links to is fire, think of it like your own little ball of sunshine. You can radiate energy out from here and you can draw it in too.

Signs the Solar Plexus is in Balance:

You'll feel your energy is good and balanced, it may fluctuate but in the whole it feels good and you have ways to bring balance back when needed. You feel in control but not controlling, you recognise your own part in things and the role that you and others have to play. You feel able to deal with life well in general and that you are in command of your own body and are actively engaged with life.

Your willpower, your energy and focus are balanced and fair. It's like you are directing the flow, the course of action, rather than cracking the whip and controlling people and situations. It is being aware of the intention and then taking the required action to make that intention a reality.

In harmony with the Solar Plexus you'll notice:

- Your energy levels are good
- You have healthy boundaries at work, at home and socially
- You can take calculated risks and can focus to get the job done
- You have a pretty good self image and a good degree of self confidence
- You'll have a good sense of humour and attitude to life in general
- You may have a particularly good gut instinct and a strong intuition
- People may be drawn to you and like being around you

Common Signs of Third Chakra Imbalance:

Imbalances can come about in many ways, here though, your boundaries are important. Boundaries allow some things in and keep some things out, whether we are talking physical, mental or emotional. If you allow a sneaky low level thought into your mind it can gnaw away at you in all sorts of ways, much like a virus, it can weaken your system. When you take in something good, it can positively feed and protect you.

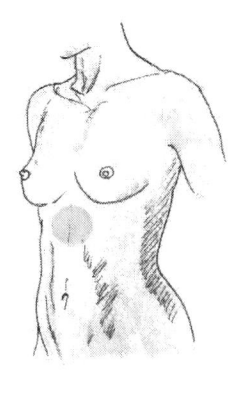

Your Solar Plexus is your main energy hub, almost your battery, and the store house of power. A bit like an energy bank. For a while we can get away with giving energy out but we also have to be aware we need to put energy back in. We can take on too much and be leeching out energy in all directions and if you have good, strong energy, you may find you attract others who inadvertently feed off your energy, even if they don't realise they're doing it. You may find you are very sensitive and as a result may suffer from various allergies. You might find that you feel drained by people and situations.

Digestive issues, stomach problems of any kind will have an impact on this chakra as will gall bladder, liver and pancreatic symptoms.

Underactive Solar Plexus Energy:

- Feeling lethargic
- Low self esteem/poor self image
- Poor self confidence
- A victim mentality or often blaming others for things
- Finding it hard to motivate yourself
- Prone to putting on weight, particularly around the mid section
- Digestive problems

Overactive Solar Plexus Energy:

- A controlling personality
- Super ambitious, a 'driven' mentality
- An over confident attitude, bordering on arrogance
- Liver problems/stomach ulcers
- Self centred with a long list of people and things you " can't stomach"
- A tendency to take on too many projects at once and rarely completing them

Bringing Balance to the Solar Plexus:

This chakra links with your ego, your personality, the person you are on a day to day basis in this modern world. We all tend to use different words to describe things but for me, this part of you is more than your personality, when it merges with your unique energy it is your soul or your soul personality.

This is the combination of your body, your mind, your emotions and your energy. (It differs from pure spirit energy as that is energy without the blessings or constraints of the human body, our soul energy is made from pure spirit energy but it has all the added experiences added to it that are manipulated and moulded by our daily lives). This soul personality is the energy we read in the aura which is fed by your chakras. Any imbalance in energy, regardless of its cause will reveal itself in the aura and this is how the energy between the soul and the spirit differ, as the spirit energy is always beautiful and pure.

To Increase Power in Your Solar Plexus:

- If you identify with some of the symptoms of a weakened Solar Plexus, any confidence building work will obviously be of use, so will some ego strengthening techniques. A good sense of self identity allows us to be positively assertive and not so affected or swayed by other people's opinions
- Find techniques and strategies to improve your own self worth and value
- Improve your decisiveness; this can be a great solar plexus boost
- Acquire the art of saying No (appropriately of course!)
- Try and keep the things in mind that motivate you, so you can focus on your goals and targets better
- Stomach exercises will naturally strengthen the solar plexus area - Pilates and Yoga are particularly good as they focus on your inner core, the muscles that surround the spine. The plank pose is a great strengthening exercise
- Boost and protect yourself energetically - using intention and visualisation, especially when you are around the energy vampires, who seem to leave you feeling drained and exhausted

To Calm an Overactive Solar Plexus Energy;

If you have dominant or controlling characteristics, take steps to work with that, either through self help or professional therapies. (Generally speaking, the people this is relevant to, do not tend to question themselves, as they instinctively decide they're always right, so will no doubt never find themselves reading this anyway!)

- Try sitting still occasionally, without a to do list in your hand and without distractions of the radio or TV (it's not that easy!)
- If you have stomach ulcers or acidic problems, avoid caffeine as much as possible
- Use gentle exercises to calm your energy, so you're still moving but the movements are more focused and deliberate, requiring you to concentrate on the muscles and generally slow down
- Try meditations and guided visualisations to keep your busy mind busy with learning to relax!
- Take notice of the silent signals your body is giving you. Although the Sacral Chakra is the emotional centre, it is here, in the Solar Plexus that you can physically feel those emotions. The adrenal glands, above the kidneys are linked to your fight or flight system and it's in the pit of your stomach you feel the desperate churnings of fear, dislike and distrust as well as the butterflies of anticipation and excitement.
- The stubborn and heavy emotions of guilt and shame can seem to hover and almost fester in this particular energy centre. Whatever you can do on a personal level to accept and deal with past events and situations, will help your energy too. Although it can seem trivial, writing or talking about such issues can bring understanding and closure.
- It's important not to force forgiveness, or to feel obliged to give it. (In fact I don't think it's something we give, forgiveness to me describes something that happens, rather than something we do or have possession of to give). Start with understanding, get clarity maybe, then let the rest

follow. Working with a trained professional for help will always make sense if and when it feels right for you.

6 CLOSED OR OPEN TO LOVE?

The Heart Chakra or Fourth Chakra

It's no surprise that this chakra is all about love. However it is not just about the love for other people, it's about our own self love, self acceptance and self kindness. It's about the inner child, the child within and your sense of compassion in general. More than any other this energy centre requires balance as it is the bridge between the upper and lower chakras, the pathway between the body and the mind.

There is evidence that the heart has a profound and unique affect on our bodies and our brains and **sends messages** up to the brain. It does not merely wait for the brain to send messages to *it*. Its energy field reaches out far beyond that of the brain. It is suggested that the heart almost has its own mini brain and nervous system that communicates with the greater nervous system of the body. See the resource page for links to more information.

Of course, the heart is vital to your health and wellbeing. This energy centre is not only responsible for regulating your blood and circulation, it also deals with your lungs and respiration, it helps to sustain life within the body.

In Balance with the Heart Chakra:

With harmony in this chakra centre, you'll more than likely notice a good sense of balance and harmony in your life in general. You'll be comfortable with nurturing yourself, having positive self talk and behaviours.

At the same time you'll be in a good position to be caring and compassionate to the people around you and society as a whole. You'll have no problem showing genuine generosity and kindness with no detriment to your own self worth. You'll enjoy a good degree of comfort in your life and find that you talk and act from the heart and people notice that about you.

This is the spiritual residency of your wisdom, it's more than knowledge and compassion, it's a beautiful combination of them both and so much more.

In Balance

- You'll have a caring and compassionate disposition
- You'll have an awareness and appreciation of the cycles and balance of life
- You feel at peace outdoors and have an affinity with nature/animals
- You're happy to nurture yourself and others and show empathy towards people in general
- People tend to think of you as a loyal and trusted friend
- You seem to be able to balance your thoughts and your feelings

Symptoms of Imbalance in the Heart Chakra:

As the heart is the area mainly affected here, any heart and circulation problems indicate an imbalance in the energy. Any chest complaints, lung and breathing issues, even asthma can all be signs of imbalance too. It's not just the heart area itself affected but also your upper back, your arms and hands too. There's no definitive line where one chakra ends and another one starts but the areas given are a good guide.

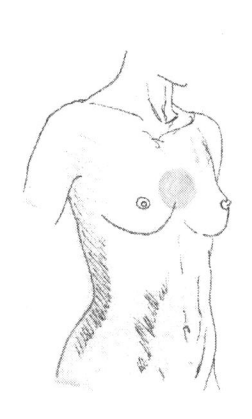

The Heart Chakra is also affected by auto immune diseases as these are to do with the body mistakenly attacking itself. Another great potential energy disruption is of course our relationships, we all know that all sorts of things can pull at our heart strings and love is not always a smooth path. It could be too much love, becoming possessive, too little, closed off to others, neediness or not feeling comfortable accepting compliments and gifts - they all can show up in the Fourth Chakra.

Underactive Heart Chakra Energy:

- Poor immune system
- Chronic allergies
- Breathing difficulties/asthma
- A resistance to intimacy or reluctance to form close bonds with people
- Poor circulation
- Feeling cut off or isolated
- A tendency to be critical, harsh or overly sarcastic with people
- Low blood pressure

Overactive Heart Chakra:

- Co dependency in your relationships might indicate an overzealous fourth chakra energy
- A jealous nature
- Some people display martyr type characteristics, always doing things for other people, quietly resenting it but neither saying nor changing anything, so it festers in the energy field
- People pleasing - regularly putting your energy into helping other people, placing their needs above yours
- High blood pressure

- When in relationships you can develop very powerful feelings very quickly, falling head over heels in love, losing yourself in your relationships

Balancing the Heart Chakra:

Air is the element associated with this chakra; it's the life force, the breath of fresh air, that makes you feel good. It has very profound connections with your spirit and when you combine love and the air you breathe you are so close to touching the beautiful energy of your spirit. We tend to take the fact we breathe for granted, which I know sounds bizarre and obvious, yet so many of us breathe so shallowly, just because we do it by default, doesn't mean we are doing it right.

There's such a spiritual connection with this chakra but for our purposes here, I'm going to try and keep to the more practical aspects as many people want something tangible and practical to start with and then are ready to move on to finding out more about our spiritual nature and meeting their own spirit and higher self. To me, trying to sum it up though, I'd say it's about falling in love with life, knowing your spirit, appreciating your physical form and the ability we all have to create our lives as we would have them be. You dance with the divine consciousness that connects us all.

Having an attitude of gratitude is a popular expression and it's also a great way of opening the flow of energy within the Heart Chakra. Noticing and acknowledging the many tiny things we have to be thankful for each day is something we are all capable of, yet can easily forget to do.

Try talking more about your appreciation of things and certainly of people. Let them know how good they make you feel, comment on their positive traits and acknowledge your own. Far too often we can see kindness as a weakness almost and we hold back on sharing simple thoughts and feelings.

Working with your inner child can be very revealing and healing. It is a large topic in itself and I have already had requests to write about this more as it's the sort of thing that crops up in my readings and healing sessions quite a lot. For now, to briefly sum it up:

Inside us all we have our child within, which holds onto our thoughts, beliefs and experiences whilst growing up. He or she is also intricately linked with your subconscious mind and can therefore be influencing a lot of your everyday behaviours and attitudes. What tends to happen is as we become adults, we push that child aside, locking them away, but if there is unfinished business of some kind then they may need, at the very least acknowledging, possibly some kind of healing and expression. This is of course very specific to the individual; there definitely is not one size that fits all.

 Any mention of the heart and it's not too long before the word forgiveness is mentioned. Forgiveness again is unique and the most important thing is you do what works for you, in a time and manner that fits. Instant 'surface' forgiveness, forgives no-one. It can be easy to say the words but only you will know if that accompanying weight has been lifted. It doesn't happen overnight, it can be a long process but just being willing to forgive can be a start. Having someone to be able to honestly talk to about the offending issue can certainly help get clarity as our feelings don't tend to come in tidy, single packages, they're usually pretty jumbled up on top of each other, some good, some bad and some indifferent.

I've found that finding out more about the energy trapped in painful memories and events can help move you nearer to that place where you are able to think about genuine forgiveness. Being outdoors is a great balancer for the Heart Chakra as it is linked with nature. The colour associated with this centre is green, the colour of Mother Nature herself. Nature allows you to be very 'present moment', it has no pretences, it just is what is and does what it does. When we can rest in the moment - even just for a short while, the heart can find peace. In our normal busy lives, it's very easy for the mind to overshadow the heart by creating worries about the future and concerns about the past.

For a few short minutes, try to be aware of where you are, purely at that point in time. I find doing this out on a walk, brings great peace and pleasure. It's a bit like sharing the moment with yourself, a conscious acknowledgement of what you are seeing and feeling. Don't walk with your head down, walk (on your own) and take notice of the scenery, the shapes, the textures, the colours, the noises, notice just how many shades of green there are.

A great reminder we used in a workshop, is to ask the question "where are my feet?" this instantly brings me to the moment and I can pause, take note of where I am, the people and situation and can then bring total awareness to whatever is going on. This sounds really simple but when we get caught up in events and situations we can be acting on automatic pilot almost and not fully embodied. It's not that easy to do, it's not so bad when you're in a quiet place on your own but add in a few work colleagues, family members or stressful situations and it becomes much more difficult to do.

The colour green is a very restful and healing colour. Using associated crystals or the colour itself can help bring in the healing calmness of this vibration. If you want to work with your own self love then pink is the colour to use and rose quartz is a lovely crystal to use too.

Practise some deep breathing exercises. We tend not to use the full capacity of our lungs. Learning to breathe deeply into them brings many benefits to your energy on every level. In our deep relaxation classes, we tend to breathe in for a count of three, pause, and then slowly exhale, to the count of six. This can be very relaxing to the body in general. If you can't manage this count, try breathing in for 2 and out for 4, then work your way up.

There are lots of different breathing techniques, experiment with some to find which ones you enjoy. These are easy to fit into your day as we tend to breathe quite a lot! And a few minutes deep breathing, on the train or drive to work could be a great way to start. In hypnosis, a large part of our work is of course related to breathing in specific ways to bring about a relaxed and peaceful state. It can work wonders and has many health benefits.

The cobra and fish pose in yoga can help the flow of energies within and around the Heart Chakra.

7 WHAT'S YOUR THROAT CHAKRA REALLY SAYING?

The Throat Chakra

Here at the throat, your energy is all about truthful communication and expression. It's about taking the energy up from your lower chakras, breathing life and love from your heart into the will and focus of your desires and now finding a way to express that energy out to the wider world.

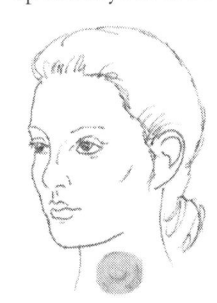

Your Throat Chakra links with your power and will from the Solar Plexus as it is here you can express yourself, speak your terms, honestly stand your ground, or you might defer and bend to the will and demands of others around you.

This is also a centre of change and works alongside the Sacral Chakra as again your emotions and creativity require honest expression, otherwise the energy becomes obstructed, twisted or stuck - tongue tied in effect.

Even if you don't think of yourself as being particularly creative, by being human you are naturally a creative being, you don't have to be an artist by trade. We ponder, we consider and we invent all the time - even if it's just a new sandwich filling or a new way of wearing the latest fashion accessory.

Indicators the Throat Chakra is in Balance:

Being about communication, this chakra obviously deals with your voice, your speech, your tone, it's about how effectively you communicate and how well you are heard and understood. Not only that, it's about how you listen and interpret others too.

In balance you'll enjoy:

- A healthy physical voice - a good tone, pitch and resonance
- Effective and congruent conversations and communication in general
- A good level of honest and supportive self talk and self expression
- Having good listening skills
- A natural capacity to flow with life and adapt to the changes that naturally evolve
- Being able to voice your opinions and ideas

- It's not just about your vocal expression, so your body language will be congruent and you're happy to share and display your creativity in whatever form you choose to express it

Signs the Throat Chakra is Out of Balance:

The entire neck region including the nose, ears and throat are included in the Throat Chakra energy. So any physical issue affecting these areas will also reveal itself in this energy centre.

Underactive energy:

- A timid, almost whispery speaking voice
- A fear of speaking up/out
- An avoidance of speaking honestly to people, whether that be out of shame, fear, guilt or embarrassment - keeping things in and swallowing words that need to be said can affect this energy centre
- Any problems with your hearing
- Excessive shyness
- Tonsillitis
- Thyroid problems
- An abusive partner or history of abuse can reveal itself in the throat chakra, as it is constantly 'chipped away at'

Overactive energy:

- Gossiping or using hurtful language
- Generally speaking loudly
- Excessively talking, finding it difficult to be quiet
- Stammering or stuttering
- Unable to keep confidences
- Asthma/thyroid/gland problems
- Bullying

Practical Ways to Balance the Fifth Chakra:

It's definitely a great help here in this chakra, to start a journal or diary, writing is a valuable form of expression and a physical way of getting things out and onto the page. Writing out your thoughts and feelings, your hopes and fears can be very cathartic. Once you start, you'll be amazed at what flows out from your deepest recesses, the important thing is just to start. There's a link to Julia Cameron's book in the resource section to find out more how writing can help you.

Until you give it a go you can't fully comprehend the difference it makes. So many successful people use it as a technique for not only clearing their head and helping them work through anything that comes up but they find all sorts of great ideas and inspirations begin to flow once they start. It's amazing the amount of thoughts you have in a day and all of that is spinning around in your mind. Your mind is more than just your brain, it's the intelligence that sits in every cell in your body and the more you do to free it up the better. Also when you see things on paper you tend to get a better perspective as to what is really going on in your life.

Start expressing what you really want to say and do. This sounds really easy but for many people they find they are not clear on *what* they truly want. (This is why counselling and journaling can provide immense help as a lot of the time people discover they've spent their life tagging along with someone else's wishes. Ultimately this can lead to resentment and numbness, to the extreme of losing sight of your own dreams and desires and any hope that a small part of them might be possible).

Do something new and/or creative. This energy centre is about flow and expression. You don't have to be an artist, or even particularly good at whatever it is, just try something that seems like it might be fun. This is a great chance to let the inner child play and create. Does he or she want to paint, bake, dance, sculpt or sing? New things give our energy a new boost. A great place to start, if you are really stuck is to recall what you liked doing as a child and revive that pleasure now as an adult, maybe that could become your new hobby?

Think about your goals and dreams, if long term goals are too difficult think about some short term ones, what could you do, see, or visit next week? Make a list of a few things and make a real effort to do at least one of them - within the next few days.

Blue is the colour associated with this chakra and can be used for healing. Wear the colour, visualise blue energy filling and revitalising your throat. You can use blue crystals as well.

Trust is important here, finding something that is good and wholesome, that gives you faith and a sense that it is safe for you to put your trust in. This chakra has a sensitive and truthful quality to it and responds well to things with this kind of nature.

Singing is a great boost to the energy overall, but especially to the throat area. As this chakra is all about sound, you can use music or sound to bring balance. There are many practitioners offering sound therapy. Alternatively you can try using the sounds of the chakras themselves to help bring balance - use mantras to focus your mind and to bring a harmony to your chakra energy. There are many things you can try - what matters is that it feels right and comfortable for you. It may seem strange but the Throat Chakra doesn't always need angelic music and mantras, sometimes a good old blast of your favourite pop or rock song will do wonders for shifting stagnant energy!

8 THE THIRD EYE. PSYCHIC, CRAZY OR WISE?

The Third Eye Chakra

This chakra is where many people focus a lot of their time and energy, hoping they will suddenly become more psychic overnight. People can appear very vague and seem to lose a grip on reality. Which, to be honest, can often be the reality of what is going on. However, this energy centre *is* about us gaining a sense of awareness to our true potential and what it means to be a human spirit. We **can** work with the energy here to become more sensitive to our intuitions and be better able to interpret the signals we are being given.

You don't have to act weird to be psychic. We all have the

ability and you can improve your own psychic ability by paying it more attention in a grounded and practical way. Psychic to me, after all is just an ability to understand and converse with energy. It is no more mystical than that and you can certainly learn more about it if you are so inclined.

Indicators of the Third Eye/Sixth Chakra in Balance:

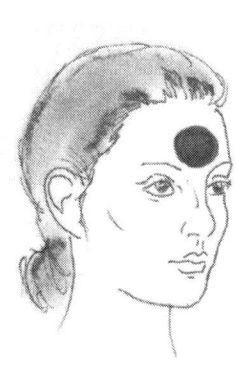

As we travel up through the energy centres, we arrive at the doorway to knowledge, wisdom and understanding. As ever, it's about balance. The awareness here allows you to see the bigger picture, your part in all things. You understand the ego's role and functions, you adapt an attitude of responsibility and humility, a respect for yourself and journey as well as that of others.

To perceive is one of the key words here, as is command. This is about seeing, understanding and determining what needs to be done. One of the ways we gain command is by working with the images of our mind and not letting our thoughts run away with themselves. Just as with breathing, we can consciously control our thoughts and can choose to feed it positively or let it feast by default, letting it gorge on worries, doubts and fears. Working with this principle is how it becomes possible for you to create the life you want.

This isn't about performing a magic spell, doing it once and 'hocus pocus' you have the dream car and mansion on the beach. This is about every day understanding the human nature, the body, the mind and the spirit. It's about feeding yourself images and learning appropriate skills to be able to create more experiences every day that you can enjoy and have more of what you desire in your life. Rather than blindly live a life in the dark, waiting for some other misguided soul who doesn't know the way either to guide you.

Your mind will bring about for real, the images and sensations you consistently give it. If your mind is full of worries and concerns, 'what ifs' and 'maybes' then you will constantly be faced with situations and events that evoke those feelings in you.

In Harmony with the Third Eye You'll Notice:

- A quiet confidence and good attitude to the world
- An active and balanced imagination - it's creative but not hallucinatory
- You're able to visualise well and hold images in your mind
- People might comment on your charismatic aura & persona
- You are fully present and grounded yet you also have a good vision for future scenarios
- You have a good memory and are able to retain facts
- You have good instincts and regularly follow your intuitive hunches
- You appreciate the universal laws of abundance, flow and energy

Imbalance in the Sixth Chakra:

It's easy for us to fall victim to stress and tension, confusion and overwhelm. All of these affect the Third Eye energy. There are all sorts of indicators but headaches and eye strain are all common symptoms here. You may also recognise some of the following:

Underactive energy:

- Difficulty visualising
- You have trouble using your imagination
- There can be a denial of events and situations, refusing to deal with issues
- You might have a fixation with the physical body, deciding that the here and now is all there is to life
- A doubting and sceptical nature, doubting anything you can't see or touch

Overactive energy:

- Frightening dreams and nightmares
- Post traumatic stress/ recurring distressing memories
- Generally having an obsessive nature
- An over active imagination
- A busy mind, finding it hard to concentrate on one thing at a time
- A tendency to live in 'fantasy land' , 'floating off' rather than being able to deal with life
- Migraines and headaches

Practical Tips to Balance the Third Eye:

One way of bringing lasting balance to this chakra (as well as boosting the others at the same time) is to develop your ability to 'see the bigger picture'. As we move up the chakra system, you naturally bring in the other elements of each successive chakra, so that your life and energy become more balanced as a whole.

Refuse to get caught up in what I call 'Soap Opera Logic' - which is what so many people do. It's all finger pointing, blaming, mistrust and denial. Aim for honesty, fairness and achieving happiness. Ditch the fixation on details that don't really matter and concern yourself less with all the things you don't want and like and spend more time thinking about how you want things to be.

Throughout the day check in with yourself, are you nurturing yourself, are you being your own best friend? Are you making yourself important, taking responsibility for your own health, wealth and happiness? All that you would do for your best friend or beloved family member are you doing for yourself too?

An attitude of compassion, fairness and gratitude can shift so many things and bring balance and harmony in all sorts of wonderful ways. Things seem to trouble you less, you let go of what doesn't matter. You have a quiet wisdom about you that permeates everything you do.

Make an effort to think about your decisions. Do you make them well, do you procrastinate, do you hesitate? Do you make your decisions out of habit, fear, in a hurry or from a balanced viewpoint, seeing further than the immediate concern? Are you asking yourself the right questions, ones that will help you move forward if stuck? So much of the time we can't see our way out of a problem, when instead of asking "why does this always happen to me?", if we asked "what's the best thing I can do about this?" or "how can I make this easier?" even "how can I make this more enjoyable?" we would find that we come up with more useful answers, opening up new avenues of possibility.

The Sixth Chakra is about understanding ourselves, and to achieve balance we want to put ourselves in the best position possible. This is about taking time to look at your own thoughts, beliefs, habits and concerns, really taking time to evaluate you, your life and how you want to live it. It is more than 'living by default' and thinking things are the way they are and you have no choice or say in the matter.

Balance is an important element to all the chakras and particularly so in these upper most centres. Try taking up Pilates, Tai Chi, Yoga or a specific class to improve your balance.

The colour purple or indigo aligns with the Third Eye. So using the same colour or crystals for balance and healing can be worthwhile - amethyst is very popular. These can also be good to use for 'psychic protection' - so if you ever feel challenged or vulnerable, visualise a purple sword, flame, pyramid or bubble around you.

Depending on the nature of the imbalance, sometimes, I'll use the opposite colour in the spectrum, to bring energy and balance. So for the Third Eye, I may use yellow for example and for the Throat Chakra I might feel that orange will be most useful. Working with energy doesn't have fixed rules, it has guidelines but the overriding factor is your feeling and intuition and an instinctive knowing what is required. Initially it is good to have some basic guidelines or principles and then experiment to find out what personally works for you.

If habitually, you're not much of a risk taker, try coming out of your comfort zone, just taking baby steps at first.

Get in the habit of trying something new, many of us eat the same foods the majority of the time, we wear a small percentage of our wardrobe, we even park our cars in the same place or sit in the same chair. Although making tiny changes can seem insignificant, if you do enough of them, you go beyond what is called the 'tipping point'. Then your 'average day' is no longer average.

Meditation and visualisation work well with all of the energy centres but especially so here. Join a meditation class or listen to a guided recording at home. This can be a beautiful way to restore balance and peace to your body, mind and spirit. (The resource page has a link to my website, which you will find updated with new recordings, so be sure to bookmark it and add it to your favourites).

Keeping a dream diary can be enlightening, even if you can't recall much at first. Make it your intention to write about them in the morning as you wake, you will soon start to recall them much more. After a while you might be able to make more sense of them and even spot of few synchronicities.

Think about how you would want your life to be. Create a **clear and definite image** of it. Cut out pictures if you can't visualise too well. Look at them regularly. Collect images that make you feel good and happy. Keep them obvious and look at them often. By doing this, you will recreate those feelings for real. (The mind cannot distinguish between a real and imagined event - it will make all sorts of chemical and minute changes whether it sees a real event or an imagined one.) The more emotion you can bring to your images the better, don't just imagine the object you want for example, imagine the outcome, the visceral experience of having it, how will you feel, what will you do, etc? This gives your manifestation ability more oomph and power, it's the super fuel required to make things happen.

Visit places or do things that create a sense of awe, wonder and beauty in your life. Appreciate the little things in life as well as the big things. Our third eye can be so blocked and 'dumbed down' by being just too 'clever' at times. By that I mean, thinking, planning, intellectualising and so on; when what it really needs is to rest, it feeds on expanding horizons, beautiful scenery and the like. It is after all, often at such times that your greatest inspirations and ideas can make themselves heard. The busy noise of everyday life can be just too loud for that quiet voice within, until you get more used to listening for it.

9 ARE YOU SUFFERING FROM A SENSE OF DISCONNECTION?

The Crown Chakra

This topmost chakra, positioned right at the top of the skull is held to be the highest energy centre. The Sixth and Seventh Chakras are where many people decide to concentrate their time and focus. However as I mentioned before, the lower chakras ideally need to be in balance and functioning well to be in the best position to work with these higher ones. This is where we really begin to balance both hemispheres of the brain and can tap into our spiritual essence and conscious connection with the wider energies around us.

The colour for this chakra is violet and sometimes white is used, signifying a pure light essence. The energy in and around the Crown Chakra can be noticeably weak in people with chronic illnesses. It gives a good indicator of the vitality and energy of the body as a whole.

The Crown Chakra in Balance:

The Crown Chakra, just as with the others, is not only about ethereal matters. It has an impact also on practical and physical levels too. It is connected with wisdom, the greater consciousness and enlightenment. However those things do not come by dissociating from everyday life. It is not about floating on some lofty cloud enjoying 'guru' status. With this chakra in balance, it is more about being able to live authentically, honouring your values, feeling your compassion, always aware that everything and everyone is connected and we all have a unique part to play.

In Balance in the Seventh Chakra You'll Enjoy:

- A deep awareness and congruence in your life
- A level of wisdom and an ability to tackle most things in life, in a calm and understanding manner, without an overpowering ego (the ego is often mentioned as being a negative thing, but it is not necessarily so)
- A charismatic personality with almost a magical quality at times
- An open mind, free to question and evaluate

- You are able to take in information, good mental faculties, an expanded mind rather than a fixed and contracted one
- An enjoyment and satisfaction in learning

Symptoms of Imbalance in the Crown Chakra:

There are lots of potential issues that can indicate imbalance, from physical things such as headaches, balance issues, traumas etc to confusion and disorientation. Anything that impacts upon the functions of the brain or the head area itself. None of the chakras are totally exclusive or independent, they are all form part of a holistic whole and as such whatever affects the lower chakras will no doubt ripple in the crown chakra too. However below are some common symptoms:

Underactive Seventh Chakra:

- You may have a closed off or cynical approach when it comes to spiritual subjects
- You can be fixed in your opinions and not open to alternative possibilities and opinions
- Difficulty in retaining information and you find it hard learning anything new
- Depression

Overactive energy:

- You may have lost interest in day to day life
- You may feel 'floaty' & dissociated from your body
- You may feel foggy and confused on a regular basis
- Over thinking. Constantly turning issues over

- Not feeling part of things, very separate and alone despite having family and people around you
- You make attachments very easily to things and people or places, deeming them to have power, more power than you

Ways to Help Balance the Crown Chakra:

The energy here, is to do with the extraordinary inner intelligence we all have It inhabits **every single cell of the body** - not just the brain. It's this mind aspect that combines with the body and spirit to make us whole. This is the infinite intelligence and it connects with us in many ways - consciously and subconsciously.

Ways to bring balance include: anything that works with the triple aspect of mind, body and spirit. Enjoy the flow of energy within and around you, start to sense your own beautiful essence. One of the most effective ways can be to try yoga, which is all about unity. There are times in our lives when we are ready for such things and when we really 'get' them. Yoga is so much more than slow movements.

However if that is not for you, increasing your awareness of your own energy and working with the tiny signals you are constantly giving and receiving can put you more in control of your energy and its potential for healing and balance. (You have been doing this for the past few chapters).

The things we have covered so far are all about bringing this energy more into your **conscious awareness**, putting you in a much better place to understand it and work with it. From there, it's not a giant leap to make any changes in your life if that feels right. All of this is about making the language of energy a part of your vocabulary, so that you can better understand yourself and the people around you.

Attempting to see the bigger picture and to be understanding of yourself and others also helps to bring balance to this energy centre. This comes when you are not overly fixated on daily issues but are still present and functioning in normal life.

Finding ways to enjoy learning new things, stimulating your interest and your mind. Stimulation helps us to grow and yet it doesn't have to be a marathon or major challenge. Keep the brain cells and interest active, keep the spark of spirit and zest alive. They're the intangible juice that keeps you bountiful, abundant and growing, regardless of age.

Of all the chakras, meditation is especially useful for balancing the crown chakra. Let troublesome thoughts drift away - just for a while - welcome in peace and serenity - allow your mind time to rest and breathe. At peace, the mind and body can start to naturally restore balance and healing.

An attitude of acceptance can be very releasing, so any work you might need to do concerning past or troubling events in your life will be very helpful. It's about understanding the truth of what went on, releasing and finding clarity in your emotions so that they are not blocking you. If at some level you are still holding on to stuff, your energy will know about it.

As this is the uppermost chakra, it requires that the previous chakras have been attended to i.e. that you pay attention to your physical body, you flow with your passion and desires, you have the will and focus to get things done.

You honour your feelings and your heart, treating yourself and others well. You speak your truth and live by your values. You hold a positive vision and direct your mind and energy into creating and sustaining the life you have and want. In doing so the whole lot comes together as a conscious acceptance of being a spirit in a body, **living on purpose and with purpose** - you become the conscious creator of your own life in harmony with the greater consciousness and the universe.

I know this may seem a little grand but it works on a practical level too. When you honour yourself and others, acting, speaking, living fairly and justly with a compassionate and understanding nature, life flows much better for you and around you. It is not about being all 'fluffy and light' but firm and fair in your presence, able to deal with life and its changes as it evolves. Aware of your own power yet still humble in your awareness of the greater world around you.

I've noticed it requires a certain degree of guts and stamina to really work with the energy of our human spirit, it certainly is not a soft option. There is an element of honesty required that cannot be pushed aside or avoided. When you embrace all this, I believe the rewards are ours for the enjoying; we feed a much wider pool than we will ever see the sides of.

10 HOW'S YOUR AURA?

Having dealt with the individual chakras, all of that energy culminates now in the aura. It is not something separate from the energy of the chakras it is made up of that exact same energy. It's the name we give the energy usually depicted as being around the human body, but it also **includes** the body as there is energy in every single cell, muscle, organ and fibre of your being.

Just as the body is made up of lots of component parts, so it is with your auric energy. It's components may not be visible, but they **can** be felt, understood and interpreted. Such things as your hopes and fears, your emotions, even your thoughts and beliefs. They can all make themselves apparent in the energy within and around you. By and large I think we have just forgotten that this energy is there and speaks to us, it's almost like a sense we don't tend to use so much these days.

We know feelings are things we can't touch as such, but we definitely know what it feels like to be scared, or how it feels to be in love. Those **are** tangible, we get body sensations to confirm what we feel. Somebody looking on, might not get these feelings but they'll notice a change in your body language, your expression and often your energy too, even if they don't have adequate words to describe it. You can probably recall a time when you walked into a room and sensed the atmosphere or some people just seem to give you the 'creeps' - that's your aura sensing and touching theirs.

We all have the ability to sense auras and just becoming more aware of their makeup and existence, being aware of the energy around you, helps to start the process off and then as with most things in life it's just about practise. It's not as hard as you might think and you don't have to have been born from a long line of clairvoyants to do it.

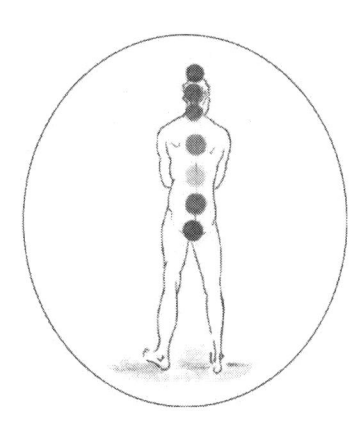

The seven main chakras we have covered so far make up your aura. Up until now we have considered them individually but just like the body, none of it works totally independently. With every breath you take an energy exchange is taking place, so your energy is continually changing and evolving.

What's in Your Aura?

Your aura is in a sense your essence; it's an energy flavour that tastes of you. What's it made from? It's made from the recipe of your life, it's all that you are, everything you have been as well as the future potential you may become. It's an energetic expression of every thought, belief and experience that relates to your life and existence. At times, certain expressions are more evident and relevant than others. It's a subtle energy that evolves with you.

That's why I like to think of it as a flavour, whatever you put in the mixing pot will affect the flavour. We are sentient emotional beings, we sing we dance, we make love and laugh. All those things that matter so much to us and have so much power to affect us don't just disappear after the experience. Your mental and emotional energy swirl around you and within you 24 - 7. The beauty is you have more control over the mixing pot than you may realise and if there's something not quite to your taste, then you have the power to change it. Take a moment now to think about what your own unique flavour might be like.

For the most part, this subtle language of energy may not have been in your conscious thoughts or awareness but on a subconscious level it always has. Working with it on a more conscious basis can be very revealing and life enhancing. Think about the last time you got really angry. To do that, your mind will recall the scene, the situation, the people involved, the words said , the actions done and importantly your body will then feel the emotions and sensations that accompanied that.

It had **energy** - you *felt* it. You can do it with any emotion, how about the last time your heart reached out to someone, bursting with love? That wasn't mindless, pointless energy, it had feeling, emotion, significance and power. It now holds a memory too, it can just be difficult to find the words to express what is going on. Although we all feel similar emotions, *how* we feel them is unique to each of us.

When people discover I can read auras, some automatically want entertaining and break into a stream of "what colour am I?", "What about my wife, what colour is she?" To me that kind of misses the point. To talk of the aura as a pretty coloured bubble that hovers around us detracts from its true substance and significance and is dismissive in a way of its beauty and profound nature. It's so much more than that.

It's also more than just being about colour. There are a great many aura colour potentials and often it's not one fixed colour, it's a mix of those given chakra colours, some will display more dominantly than others. Each colour reflects different aspects of your character and personality. It brings all the references and significances of its relevant chakra. And there may be other colour mutations added as well.

All of the colours have positive and negative trait potential, just as our personalities do. Being assertive for example is a nice balanced state, push it too far and that assertiveness can become aggressive and too far in the other direction you may be a bit of a pushover. To read the colour, you read the vibrancy, it may be washed out or patchy or it might be a sludgy tone, rather than the bright vibrant core colour.

There are more ways to read auras than just using colour. I usually get more from sensations, feelings and impressions. Often I'll get flashes of images and sometimes entire scenes play out. It's almost like watching little video clips which I then relay to the client. We all have the ability to do this, I am no different from you. I think the biggest sticking point is the fear of not saying what you see, as the images don't always make sense to us and we expect far too much detail in the beginning - so we don't start. What I found is when I just say what I see, it seems to start a dialogue and that's when the play button gets pressed and more of the story unfolds.

Sometimes the energy can feel cold or hot, cobwebby or clammy. These can indicate ill health or an energy imbalance, which might relate to a current problem, an old surgery or a more thought based or emotional issue. Once again, how we each sense things is slightly different for all of us. It's a bit like having a different accent in languages. Well the language of energy is no different, your accent may be different to mine and it doesn't make either of us right or wrong. It's just different. As you work with it though, you move on from learning the basic alphabet and develop your own fluency and style.

Get beyond the surface and the 'colour' of the aura and you realise that both it and you, your entire body in fact is a reflection of your innermost thoughts, experiences, emotions and beliefs. It permeates your body, mind and spirit.

Learning to decipher and interpret the energetic language patterns, you can start to better understand the people and events in your life and even your own physical health, habits and tendencies. Then it's a matter of deciding what, if anything you'd like to do about it. Maybe there will be things that need addressing and dealing with, some might need clearing away and releasing. Some of the energy you carry might not even be yours!

You then are in a better place to focus the energy of your mind and your thoughts to invite more of what you do want into your life. Living on purpose and with purpose, rather than by default just because that is what it seems everyone else is doing!

To me it's not a question of why bother with your aura and your energy - It's more like why on earth not!

RESOURCES

Facebook:

http://www.facebook.com/aurasandchakras

Twitter:

https://twitter.com/Secret_Aura

MP3 recording:

http://www.aurasandchakras.com/chakra-balancing-resources/

"How to Read Auras" by Davina DeSilver available on Amazon

Julia Cameron:"The Artist's Way"

Printed in Great Britain
by Amazon